Hello dear,

I hope you'll keep your inner child happy with this colorful journal and find it so helpful in creating your own reality.
There's nothing you can't have, do or be. Life is a beautiful journey, and you should enjoy it to the fullest.

Every day we wake up is a new chance for an amazing life. That being said we should feel grateful for each morning we've been gifted with.
If we invite GRATITUDE to our daily routine, life is going to give us more and more "things" to be grateful for.

In next few pages see an example of filling out My New Reality Journal.

Love,
Jay Venera

Date _____

I woke up today feeling grateful for:

1. _____*My family*_____

2. _____*Health*_____

3. _____*Sunny day*_____

My wish for today is _____ *to get that job I applied for three days ago* _____ and I will let universe do its thing.

Affirmations:

I am
_____*Happy*_____
_____*Beautiful*_____
_____*Loving*_____

Today _____*Maya*_____ helped me realize/learn/remember that _____*I should be more patient with myself*_____

Today I am very proud of myself for _____*having courage*_____ _____*to create something new*_____

I am going to bed grateful for today's day and:

1. _____*new job that I got*_____

2. _____*my trip to the beach*_____

3. _____*the quality time I had with my friends*_____

4. _____*the great dinner I had*_____

5. _____*new knowledge I gained*_____

Good night _____*put your name here*_____, I love you.

Beliefs that don't serve me anymore:

My life is chaotic

I don't have enough money

It's very hard to find love

New beliefs that are serving me NOW:

My life is amazing

I have enough money for everything I want and more

Love is everywhere around me and I am so loved

Page of positive aspects

Often when something we don't want is happening to (for) us, we struggle to see things from a different angle. It's not all that bad. As a matter of fact all "bad" situations are blessings in disguise.

Example:

I got fired from my job.

Positive aspects of this situation:

* I have more free time to connect better with my loved ones.

* I can dedicate myself to something I really love doing.

* There's a way better job than this one waiting for me.

Everything you can imagine is real.

Pablo Picasso

It's happening

Here you will write things you want to happen in a present tense, like it's already happening. Write a whole page. Make up new story and create your new reality. Tune into your emotions. Enliven that new story in your feelings.

Example:

I am sitting on the beach in Hawaii, drinking beautiful coconut water. My partner is with me. We are having so much fun. I have job of my dreams and enough money for everything I want and need, etc.

What do I want?
Why do I want it?

I want a new car.

I want it because it will be safer than the one I have right now.

I would like to take my mother on a road trip.

The thought of having a new car brings me peace and a sense of security, etc.

Letter to: _____

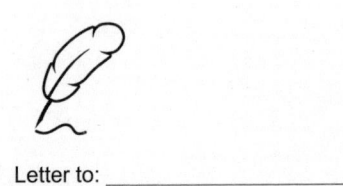

Sometimes we don't have enough courage to express our feelings to another person, or that person is not here now, or is no longer with us. Sometimes that person is you. It's very important to let it all out. You don't have to send this letter ever. Be intimate with your feelings; don't ever suppress them.

I forgive you …

Forgive them. Not because they deserve forgiveness, but because you deserve peace.

In case somebody (including yourself) has wronged you or hurt you in any way, forgive them. They simply didn't know better.

Forgive them and send them love whenever you're ready.

Date _____

I woke up today feeling grateful for:

1. _____
2. _____
3. _____

My wish for today is _____

_____ and I will let universe do its thing.

Affirmations:

I am _____

_____

_____

Today _____ helped me realize/learn/remember that _____
_____

Today I am very proud of myself for _____
_____
_____

I am going to bed grateful for today's day and:

1. _____
2. _____
3. _____
4. _____
5. _____

Good night _____, I love you.

Date _____

I woke up today feeling grateful for:

1. _____
2. _____
3. _____

My wish for today is _____

_____ and I will let universe do its thing.

Affirmations:

I am _____

_____

_____

Today _____ helped me realize/learn/remember that _____
_____

Today I am very proud of myself for _____
_____
_____

I am going to bed grateful for today's day and:

1. _____
2. _____
3. _____
4. _____
5. _____

Good night _____, I love you.

Date _____

I woke up today feeling grateful for:

1. _____
2. _____
3. _____

My wish for today is _____

_____ and I will let universe do its thing.

Affirmations:

I am _____

_____

_____

Today _____ helped me realize/learn/remember that _____
_____

Today I am very proud of myself for _____
_____
_____

I am going to bed grateful for today's day and:

1. _____
2. _____
3. _____
4. _____
5. _____

Good night _____, I love you.

Date _____

I woke up today feeling grateful for:

1. _____

2. _____

3. _____

My wish for today is _____

_____ and I will let universe do its thing.

Affirmations:

I am _____

_____

_____

Today _____ helped me realize/learn/remember that _____
_____

Today I am very proud of myself for _____
_____
_____

I am going to bed grateful for today's day and:

1._____
2._____
3._____
4._____
5._____

Good night _____, I love you.

Date _____

I woke up today feeling grateful for:

1._____
2._____
3._____

My wish for today is _____
_____ and I will let universe do its thing.

Affirmations:

I am _____
_____
_____

Today _____ helped me realize/learn/remember

that _____

_____

Today I am very proud of myself for _____

_____

_____

I am going to bed grateful for today's day and:

1._____

2._____

3._____

4._____

5._____

Good night _____, I love you.

Date _____

I woke up today feeling grateful for:

1. _____
2. _____
3. _____

My wish for today is _____
_____ and I will let universe do its thing.

Affirmations:

I am _____
_____
_____

Today _____ helped me realize/learn/remember that _____
_____

Today I am very proud of myself for _____
_____
_____

I am going to bed grateful for today's day and:

1. _____
2. _____
3. _____
4. _____
5. _____

Good night _____, I love you.

Date _____

I woke up today feeling grateful for:

1. _____
2. _____
3. _____

My wish for today is _____

_____ and I will let universe do its thing.

Affirmations:

I am _____

_____

_____

Today _____ helped me realize/learn/remember
that _____
_____

Today I am very proud of myself for _____
_____
_____

I am going to bed grateful for today's day and:

1. _____
2. _____
3. _____
4. _____
5. _____

Good night _____, I love you.

Date _____

I woke up today feeling grateful for:

1. _____
2. _____
3. _____

My wish for today is _____

_____ and I will let universe do its thing.

Affirmations:

I am _____

_____

_____

Today _____ helped me realize/learn/remember that _____
_____

Today I am very proud of myself for _____

_____

_____

I am going to bed grateful for today's day and:

1._____

2._____

3._____

4._____

5._____

Good night _____, I love you.

Date _____

I woke up today feeling grateful for:

1. _____
2. _____
3. _____

My wish for today is _____

_____ and I will let universe do its thing.

Affirmations:

I am _____

_____

_____

Today _____ helped me realize/learn/remember that _____
_____

Today I am very proud of myself for _____
_____
_____

I am going to bed grateful for today's day and:

1. _____
2. _____
3. _____
4. _____
5. _____

Good night _____, I love you.

Date _____

I woke up today feeling grateful for:

1. _____

2. _____

3. _____

My wish for today is _____

_____ and I will let universe do its thing.

Affirmations:

I am _____

_____

_____

Today _____ helped me realize/learn/remember that _____
_____

Today I am very proud of myself for _____
_____
_____

I am going to bed grateful for today's day and:

1. _____
2. _____
3. _____
4. _____
5. _____

Good night _____, I love you.

Date _____

I woke up today feeling grateful for:

1. _____
2. _____
3. _____

My wish for today is _____

_____ and I will let universe do its thing.

Affirmations:

I am _____

_____

_____

Today _____ helped me realize/learn/remember that _____
_____

Today I am very proud of myself for _____
_____
_____

I am going to bed grateful for today's day and:

1. _____
2. _____
3. _____
4. _____
5. _____

Good night _____, I love you.

Date _____

I woke up today feeling grateful for:

1. _____
2. _____
3. _____

My wish for today is _____

_____ and I will let universe do its thing.

Affirmations:

I am _____

_____

_____

Today _____ helped me realize/learn/remember that _____

_____

Today I am very proud of myself for _____

_____

_____

I am going to bed grateful for today's day and:

1. _____
2. _____
3. _____
4. _____
5. _____

Good night _____, I love you.

Date _____

I woke up today feeling grateful for:

1. _____
2. _____
3. _____

My wish for today is _____
_____ and I will let universe do its thing.

Affirmations:

I am _____
_____
_____

Today _____ helped me realize/learn/remember

that _____

_____

Today I am very proud of myself for _____

_____

_____

I am going to bed grateful for today's day and:

1._____

2._____

3._____

4._____

5._____

Good night _____, I love you.

Date _____

I woke up today feeling grateful for:

1. _____

2. _____

3. _____

My wish for today is _____

_____ and I will let universe do its thing.

Affirmations:

I am _____

_____

_____

Today _____ helped me realize/learn/remember

that _____

_____

Today I am very proud of myself for _____

_____

_____

I am going to bed grateful for today's day and:

1._____

2._____

3._____

4._____

5._____

Good night _____, I love you.

Date _____

I woke up today feeling grateful for:

1. _____
2. _____
3. _____

My wish for today is _____

_____ and I will let universe do its thing.

Affirmations:

I am _____

_____

_____

Today _____ helped me realize/learn/remember that _____
_____

Today I am very proud of myself for _____
_____
_____

I am going to bed grateful for today's day and:

1._____
2._____
3._____
4._____
5._____

Good night _____, I love you.

Date _____

I woke up today feeling grateful for:

1. _____
2. _____
3. _____

My wish for today is _____

_____ and I will let universe do its thing.

Affirmations:

I am _____

_____

_____

Today _____ helped me realize/learn/remember that _____
_____

Today I am very proud of myself for _____
_____
_____

I am going to bed grateful for today's day and:

1. _____
2. _____
3. _____
4. _____
5. _____

Good night _____, I love you.

Date _____

I woke up today feeling grateful for:

1. _____
2. _____
3. _____

My wish for today is _____

_____ and I will let universe do its thing.

Affirmations:

I am _____

_____

_____

Today _____ helped me realize/learn/remember that _____
_____

Today I am very proud of myself for _____
_____
_____

I am going to bed grateful for today's day and:

1. _____
2. _____
3. _____
4. _____
5. _____

Good night _____, I love you.

Date _____

I woke up today feeling grateful for:

1. _____
2. _____
3. _____

My wish for today is _____

_____ and I will let universe do its thing.

Affirmations:

I am _____

_____

_____

Today _____ helped me realize/learn/remember

that _____

_____

Today I am very proud of myself for _____

_____

_____

I am going to bed grateful for today's day and:

1._____

2._____

3._____

4._____

5._____

Good night _____, I love you.

Date _____

I woke up today feeling grateful for:

1. _____
2. _____
3. _____

My wish for today is _____
_____ and I will let universe do its thing.

Affirmations:

I am _____
_____
_____

Today _____ helped me realize/learn/remember that _____
_____

Today I am very proud of myself for _____
_____
_____

I am going to bed grateful for today's day and:

1. _____
2. _____
3. _____
4. _____
5. _____

Good night _____, I love you.

Date _____

I woke up today feeling grateful for:

1. _____
2. _____
3. _____

My wish for today is _____

_____ and I will let universe do its thing.

Affirmations:

I am _____
_____
_____

Today _____ helped me realize/learn/remember that _____
_____

Today I am very proud of myself for _____
_____
_____

I am going to bed grateful for today's day and:

1. _____
2. _____
3. _____
4. _____
5. _____

Good night _____, I love you.

Date _____

I woke up today feeling grateful for:

1. _____
2. _____
3. _____

My wish for today is _____

_____ and I will let universe do its thing.

Affirmations:

I am _____

_____

_____

Today _____ helped me realize/learn/remember that _____
_____

Today I am very proud of myself for _____
_____
_____

I am going to bed grateful for today's day and:

1._____

2._____

3._____

4._____

5._____

Good night _____, I love you.

Date _____

I woke up today feeling grateful for:

1. _____

2. _____

3. _____

My wish for today is _____

_____ and I will let universe do its thing.

Affirmations:

I am _____

_____

_____

Today _____ helped me realize/learn/remember that _____
_____

Today I am very proud of myself for _____
_____
_____

I am going to bed grateful for today's day and:

1. _____
2. _____
3. _____
4. _____
5. _____

Good night _____, I love you.

Date _____

I woke up today feeling grateful for:

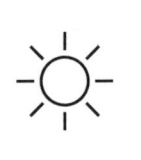

1._____
2._____
3._____

My wish for today is _____
_____ and I will let universe do its thing.

Affirmations:

I am _____
_____
_____

Today _____ helped me realize/learn/remember that _____
_____

Today I am very proud of myself for _____

_____

_____

I am going to bed grateful for today's day and:

1._____

2._____

3._____

4._____

5._____

Good night _____, I love you.

Date _____

I woke up today feeling grateful for:

1._____

2._____

3._____

My wish for today is _____

_____ and I will let universe do its thing.

Affirmations:

I am _____

_____

_____

Today _____ helped me realize/learn/remember

that _____

_____

Today I am very proud of myself for _____

_____

_____

I am going to bed grateful for today's day and:

1. _____

2. _____

3. _____

4. _____

5. _____

Good night _____, I love you.

Date _____

I woke up today feeling grateful for:

1. _____

2. _____

3. _____

My wish for today is _____

_____ and I will let universe do its thing.

Affirmations:

I am _____

_____

_____

Today _____ helped me realize/learn/remember that _____
_____

Today I am very proud of myself for _____
_____
_____

I am going to bed grateful for today's day and:

1. _____
2. _____
3. _____
4. _____
5. _____

Good night _____, I love you.

Date _____

I woke up today feeling grateful for:

1. _____
2. _____
3. _____

My wish for today is _____

_____ and I will let universe do its thing.

Affirmations:

I am _____

_____

_____

Today _____ helped me realize/learn/remember that _____
_____

Today I am very proud of myself for _____

_____

_____

I am going to bed grateful for today's day and:

1. _____
2. _____
3. _____
4. _____
5. _____

Good night _____, I love you.

Date _____

I woke up today feeling grateful for:

1. _____
2. _____
3. _____

My wish for today is _____
_____ and I will let universe do its thing.

Affirmations:

I am _____
_____
_____

Today _____ helped me realize/learn/remember that _____
_____

Today I am very proud of myself for _____
_____
_____

I am going to bed grateful for today's day and:

1. _____
2. _____
3. _____
4. _____
5. _____

Good night _____, I love you.

Date _____

I woke up today feeling grateful for:

1. _____
2. _____
3. _____

My wish for today is _____

_____ and I will let universe do its thing.

Affirmations:

I am _____

_____

_____

Today _____ helped me realize/learn/remember that _____
_____

Today I am very proud of myself for _____

_____

_____

I am going to bed grateful for today's day and:

1._____

2._____

3._____

4._____

5._____

Good night _____, I love you.

Date _____

I woke up today feeling grateful for:

1. _____
2. _____
3. _____

My wish for today is _____

_____ and I will let universe do its thing.

Affirmations:

I am _____
_____
_____

Today _____ helped me realize/learn/remember that _____
_____

Today I am very proud of myself for _____
_____
_____

I am going to bed grateful for today's day and:

1. _____
2. _____
3. _____
4. _____
5. _____

Good night _____, I love you.

Date _____

I woke up today feeling grateful for:

1. _____
2. _____
3. _____

My wish for today is _____

_____ and I will let universe do its thing.

Affirmations:

I am _____

_____

_____

Today _____ helped me realize/learn/remember that _____
_____

Today I am very proud of myself for _____
_____
_____

I am going to bed grateful for today's day and:

1._____

2._____

3._____

4._____

5._____

Good night _____, I love you.

Date _____

I woke up today feeling grateful for:

1._____

2._____

3._____

My wish for today is _____

_____ and I will let universe do its thing.

Affirmations:

I am _____

_____

_____

Today _____ helped me realize/learn/remember that _____
_____

Today I am very proud of myself for _____
_____
_____

I am going to bed grateful for today's day and:

1._____

2._____

3._____

4._____

5._____

Good night _____, I love you.

Date _____

I woke up today feeling grateful for:

1. _____
2. _____
3. _____

My wish for today is _____
_____ and I will let universe do its thing.

Affirmations:

I am _____
_____
_____

Today _____ helped me realize/learn/remember that _____
_____

Today I am very proud of myself for _____
_____
_____

I am going to bed grateful for today's day and:

1. _____
2. _____
3. _____
4. _____
5. _____

Good night _____, I love you.

Date _____

I woke up today feeling grateful for:

1. _____
2. _____
3. _____

My wish for today is _____

_____ and I will let universe do its thing.

Affirmations:

I am _____

_____

_____

Today _____ helped me realize/learn/remember that _____
_____

Today I am very proud of myself for _____
_____
_____

I am going to bed grateful for today's day and:

1. _____
2. _____
3. _____
4. _____
5. _____

Good night _____, I love you.

Date _____

I woke up today feeling grateful for:

1. _____
2. _____
3. _____

My wish for today is _____

_____ and I will let universe do its thing.

Affirmations:

I am _____

_____

_____

Today _____ helped me realize/learn/remember that _____
_____

Today I am very proud of myself for _____
_____
_____

I am going to bed grateful for today's day and:

1. _____
2. _____
3. _____
4. _____
5. _____

Good night _____, I love you.

Date _____

I woke up today feeling grateful for:

1. _____
2. _____
3. _____

My wish for today is _____
_____ and I will let universe do its thing.

Affirmations:

I am _____
_____
_____

Today _____ helped me realize/learn/remember that _____
_____

Today I am very proud of myself for _____
_____
_____

I am going to bed grateful for today's day and:

1. _____
2. _____
3. _____
4. _____
5. _____

Good night _____, I love you.

Date _____

I woke up today feeling grateful for:

1. _____
2. _____
3. _____

My wish for today is _____

_____ and I will let universe do its thing.

Affirmations:

I am _____

_____

_____

Today _____ helped me realize/learn/remember that _____
_____

Today I am very proud of myself for _____
_____
_____

I am going to bed grateful for today's day and:

1. _____
2. _____
3. _____
4. _____
5. _____

Good night _____, I love you.

Date _____

I woke up today feeling grateful for:

1. _____
2. _____
3. _____

My wish for today is _____

_____ and I will let universe do its thing.

Affirmations:

I am _____

_____

_____

Today _____ helped me realize/learn/remember that _____
_____

Today I am very proud of myself for _____
_____
_____

I am going to bed grateful for today's day and:

1. _____
2. _____
3. _____
4. _____
5. _____

Good night _____, I love you.

Date _____

I woke up today feeling grateful for:

1. _____
2. _____
3. _____

My wish for today is _____
_____ and I will let universe do its thing.

Affirmations:

I am _____
_____
_____

Today _____ helped me realize/learn/remember that _____
_____

Today I am very proud of myself for _____

_____

_____

I am going to bed grateful for today's day and:

1._____

2._____

3._____

4._____

5._____

Good night _____, I love you.

Date _____

I woke up today feeling grateful for:

1._____
2._____
3._____

My wish for today is _____
_____ and I will let universe do its thing.

Affirmations:

I am _____
_____
_____

Today _____ helped me realize/learn/remember that _____
_____

Today I am very proud of myself for _____
_____
_____

I am going to bed grateful for today's day and:

1._____

2._____

3._____

4._____

5._____

Good night _____, I love you.

Date _____

I woke up today feeling grateful for:

1. _____
2. _____
3. _____

My wish for today is _____
_____ and I will let universe do its thing.

Affirmations:

I am _____
_____
_____

Today _____ helped me realize/learn/remember
that _____
_____

Today I am very proud of myself for _____
_____
_____

I am going to bed grateful for today's day and:

1. _____
2. _____
3. _____
4. _____
5. _____

Good night _____, I love you.

Date _____

I woke up today feeling grateful for:

1. _____

2. _____

3. _____

My wish for today is _____

_____ and I will let universe do its thing.

Affirmations:

I am _____

_____

_____

Today _____ helped me realize/learn/remember

that _____

_____

Today I am very proud of myself for _____

_____

_____

I am going to bed grateful for today's day and:

1._____

2._____

3._____

4._____

5._____

Good night _____, I love you.

Date _____

I woke up today feeling grateful for:

1._____

2._____

3._____

My wish for today is _____

_____ and I will let universe do its thing.

Affirmations:

I am _____

_____

_____

Today _____ helped me realize/learn/remember that _____
_____

Today I am very proud of myself for _____
_____
_____

I am going to bed grateful for today's day and:

1. _____
2. _____
3. _____
4. _____
5. _____

Good night _____, I love you.

Date _____

I woke up today feeling grateful for:

1._____
2._____
3._____

My wish for today is _____
_____ and I will let universe do its thing.

Affirmations:

I am _____
_____
_____

Today _____ helped me realize/learn/remember that _____
_____

Today I am very proud of myself for _____
_____
_____

I am going to bed grateful for today's day and:

1. _____
2. _____
3. _____
4. _____
5. _____

Good night _____, I love you.

Date _____

I woke up today feeling grateful for:

1. _____
2. _____
3. _____

My wish for today is _____
_____ and I will let universe do its thing.

Affirmations:

I am _____
_____
_____

Today _____ helped me realize/learn/remember that _____
_____

Today I am very proud of myself for _____
_____
_____

I am going to bed grateful for today's day and:

1. _____
2. _____
3. _____
4. _____
5. _____

Good night _____, I love you.

Date _____

I woke up today feeling grateful for:

1. _____

2. _____

3. _____

My wish for today is _____

_____ and I will let universe do its thing.

Affirmations:

I am _____

_____

_____

Today _____ helped me realize/learn/remember that _____
_____

Today I am very proud of myself for _____
_____
_____

I am going to bed grateful for today's day and:

1. _____
2. _____
3. _____
4. _____
5. _____

Good night _____, I love you.

Date _____

I woke up today feeling grateful for:

1. _____
2. _____
3. _____

My wish for today is _____
_____ and I will let universe do its thing.

Affirmations:

I am _____
_____
_____

Today _____ helped me realize/learn/remember

that _____

_____

Today I am very proud of myself for _____

_____

_____

I am going to bed grateful for today's day and:

1. _____

2. _____

3. _____

4. _____

5. _____

Good night _____, I love you.

Date _____

I woke up today feeling grateful for:

1. _____
2. _____
3. _____

My wish for today is _____
_____ and I will let universe do its thing.

Affirmations:

I am _____
_____
_____

Today _____ helped me realize/learn/remember

that _____

_____

Today I am very proud of myself for _____

_____

_____

I am going to bed grateful for today's day and:

1. _____

2. _____

3. _____

4. _____

5. _____

Good night _____, I love you.

Date _____

I woke up today feeling grateful for:

1. _____

2. _____

3. _____

My wish for today is _____

_____ and I will let universe do its thing.

Affirmations:

I am _____

_____

_____

Today _____ helped me realize/learn/remember

that _____

_____

Today I am very proud of myself for _____

_____

_____

I am going to bed grateful for today's day and:

1._____

2._____

3._____

4._____

5._____

Good night _____, I love you.

Date _____

I woke up today feeling grateful for:

1. _____
2. _____
3. _____

My wish for today is _____

_____ and I will let universe do its thing.

Affirmations:

I am _____

_____

_____

Today _____ helped me realize/learn/remember that _____
_____

Today I am very proud of myself for _____
_____
_____

I am going to bed grateful for today's day and:

1. _____
2. _____
3. _____
4. _____
5. _____

Good night _____, I love you.

Date _____

I woke up today feeling grateful for:

1. _____
2. _____
3. _____

My wish for today is _____

_____ and I will let universe do its thing.

Affirmations:

I am _____

_____

_____

Today _____ helped me realize/learn/remember that _____
_____

Today I am very proud of myself for _____
_____
_____

I am going to bed grateful for today's day and:

1. _____
2. _____
3. _____
4. _____
5. _____

Good night _____, I love you.

Date _____

I woke up today feeling grateful for:

1. _____
2. _____
3. _____

My wish for today is _____

_____ and I will let universe do its thing.

Affirmations:

I am _____

_____

_____

Today _____ helped me realize/learn/remember that _____

_____

Today I am very proud of myself for _____

_____

_____

I am going to bed grateful for today's day and:

1. _____
2. _____
3. _____
4. _____
5. _____

Good night _____, I love you.

Date _____

I woke up today feeling grateful for:

1. _____
2. _____
3. _____

My wish for today is _____

_____ and I will let universe do its thing.

Affirmations:

I am _____

_____

_____

Today _____ helped me realize/learn/remember that _____
_____

Today I am very proud of myself for _____
_____
_____

I am going to bed grateful for today's day and:

1. _____
2. _____
3. _____
4. _____
5. _____

Good night _____, I love you.

Date _____

I woke up today feeling grateful for:

1._____
2._____
3._____

My wish for today is _____
_____ and I will let universe do its thing.

Affirmations:

I am _____
_____
_____

Today _____ helped me realize/learn/remember that _____
_____

Today I am very proud of myself for _____
_____
_____

I am going to bed grateful for today's day and:

1._____
2._____
3._____
4._____
5._____

Good night _____, I love you.

Date _____

I woke up today feeling grateful for:

1._____

2._____

3._____

My wish for today is _____

_____ and I will let universe do its thing.

Affirmations:

I am _____

_____

_____

Today _____ helped me realize/learn/remember

that _____

_____

Today I am very proud of myself for _____

_____

_____

I am going to bed grateful for today's day and:

1._____

2._____

3._____

4._____

5._____

Good night _____, I love you.

Date _____

I woke up today feeling grateful for:

1. _____
2. _____
3. _____

My wish for today is _____
_____ and I will let universe do its thing.

Affirmations:

I am _____
_____
_____

Today _____ helped me realize/learn/remember

that _____

_____

Today I am very proud of myself for _____

_____

_____

I am going to bed grateful for today's day and:

1. _____

2. _____

3. _____

4. _____

5. _____

Good night _____, I love you.

Date _____

I woke up today feeling grateful for:

1. _____
2. _____
3. _____

My wish for today is _____
_____ and I will let universe do its thing.

Affirmations:

I am _____
_____
_____

Today _____ helped me realize/learn/remember that _____
_____

Today I am very proud of myself for _____
_____
_____

I am going to bed grateful for today's day and:

1._____

2._____

3._____

4._____

5._____

Good night _____, I love you.

Date _____

I woke up today feeling grateful for:

1. _____
2. _____
3. _____

My wish for today is _____
_____ and I will let universe do its thing.

Affirmations:

I am _____
_____
_____

Today _____ helped me realize/learn/remember that _____
_____

Today I am very proud of myself for _____
_____
_____

I am going to bed grateful for today's day and:

1. _____
2. _____
3. _____
4. _____
5. _____

Good night _____, I love you.

Date _____

I woke up today feeling grateful for:

1. _____
2. _____
3. _____

My wish for today is _____

_____ and I will let universe do its thing.

Affirmations:

I am _____

_____

_____

Today _____ helped me realize/learn/remember that _____
_____

Today I am very proud of myself for _____
_____
_____

I am going to bed grateful for today's day and:

1. _____
2. _____
3. _____
4. _____
5. _____

Good night _____, I love you.

Date _____

I woke up today feeling grateful for:

1. _____

2. _____

3. _____

My wish for today is _____

_____ and I will let universe do its thing.

Affirmations:

I am _____

_____

_____

Today _____ helped me realize/learn/remember that _____
_____

Today I am very proud of myself for _____
_____
_____

I am going to bed grateful for today's day and:

1. _____
2. _____
3. _____
4. _____
5. _____

Good night _____, I love you.

Date _____

I woke up today feeling grateful for:

1. _____
2. _____
3. _____

My wish for today is _____

_____ and I will let universe do its thing.

Affirmations:

I am _____

_____

_____

Today _____ helped me realize/learn/remember that _____

_____

Today I am very proud of myself for _____

_____

_____

I am going to bed grateful for today's day and:

1. _____
2. _____
3. _____
4. _____
5. _____

Good night _____, I love you.

Date _____

I woke up today feeling grateful for:

1._____

2._____

3._____

My wish for today is _____

_____ and I will let universe do its thing.

Affirmations:

I am _____

_____

_____

Today _____ helped me realize/learn/remember that _____
_____

Today I am very proud of myself for _____
_____
_____

I am going to bed grateful for today's day and:

1. _____
2. _____
3. _____
4. _____
5. _____

Good night _____, I love you.

Date _____

I woke up today feeling grateful for:

1. _____
2. _____
3. _____

My wish for today is _____

_____ and I will let universe do its thing.

Affirmations:

I am _____

_____

_____

Today _____ helped me realize/learn/remember

that _____

_____

Today I am very proud of myself for _____

_____

_____

I am going to bed grateful for today's day and:

1._____

2._____

3._____

4._____

5._____

Good night _____, I love you.

Date _____

I woke up today feeling grateful for:

1._____

2._____

3._____

My wish for today is _____

_____ and I will let universe do its thing.

Affirmations:

I am _____

_____

_____

Today _____ helped me realize/learn/remember

that _____

_____

Today I am very proud of myself for _____

_____

_____

I am going to bed grateful for today's day and:

1. _____

2. _____

3. _____

4. _____

5. _____

Good night _____, I love you.

Date _____

I woke up today feeling grateful for:

1. _____
2. _____
3. _____

My wish for today is _____
_____ and I will let universe do its thing.

Affirmations:

I am _____
_____
_____

Today _____ helped me realize/learn/remember that _____
_____

Today I am very proud of myself for _____
_____
_____

I am going to bed grateful for today's day and:

1. _____
2. _____
3. _____
4. _____
5. _____

Good night _____, I love you.

Date _____

I woke up today feeling grateful for:

1. _____
2. _____
3. _____

My wish for today is _____

_____ and I will let universe do its thing.

Affirmations:

I am _____

_____

_____

Today _____ helped me realize/learn/remember that _____
_____

Today I am very proud of myself for _____
_____
_____

I am going to bed grateful for today's day and:

1._____
2._____
3._____
4._____
5._____

Good night _____, I love you.

Date _____

I woke up today feeling grateful for:

1._____
2._____
3._____

My wish for today is _____

_____ and I will let universe do its thing.

Affirmations:

I am _____

_____

_____

Today _____ helped me realize/learn/remember

that _____

_____

Today I am very proud of myself for _____

_____

_____

I am going to bed grateful for today's day and:

1. _____

2. _____

3. _____

4. _____

5. _____

Good night _____, I love you.

Date _____

I woke up today feeling grateful for:

1. _____
2. _____
3. _____

My wish for today is _____

_____ and I will let universe do its thing.

Affirmations:

I am _____
_____
_____

Today _____ helped me realize/learn/remember that _____
_____

Today I am very proud of myself for _____
_____
_____

I am going to bed grateful for today's day and:

1. _____
2. _____
3. _____
4. _____
5. _____

Good night _____, I love you.

Date _____

I woke up today feeling grateful for:

1._____
2._____
3._____

My wish for today is _____

_____ and I will let universe do its thing.

Affirmations:

I am _____

_____

_____

Today _____ helped me realize/learn/remember that _____
_____

Today I am very proud of myself for _____
_____
_____

I am going to bed grateful for today's day and:

1. _____
2. _____
3. _____
4. _____
5. _____

Good night _____, I love you.

Date _____

I woke up today feeling grateful for:

1._____
2._____
3._____

My wish for today is _____
_____ and I will let universe do its thing.

Affirmations:

I am _____
_____
_____

Today _____ helped me realize/learn/remember

that _____

_____

Today I am very proud of myself for _____

_____

_____

I am going to bed grateful for today's day and:

1._____

2._____

3._____

4._____

5._____

Good night _____, I love you.

Date _____

I woke up today feeling grateful for:

1._____
2._____
3._____

My wish for today is _____

_____ and I will let universe do its thing.

Affirmations:

I am _____

_____

_____

Today _____ helped me realize/learn/remember that _____
_____

Today I am very proud of myself for _____
_____
_____

I am going to bed grateful for today's day and:

1._____
2._____
3._____
4._____
5._____

Good night _____, I love you.

Date _____

I woke up today feeling grateful for:

1._____
2._____
3._____

My wish for today is _____

_____ and I will let universe do its thing.

Affirmations:

I am _____

_____

_____

Today _____ helped me realize/learn/remember that _____
_____

Today I am very proud of myself for _____
_____
_____

I am going to bed grateful for today's day and:

1. _____
2. _____
3. _____
4. _____
5. _____

Good night _____, I love you.

Date _____

I woke up today feeling grateful for:

1. _____
2. _____
3. _____

My wish for today is _____
_____ and I will let universe do its thing.

Affirmations:

I am _____
_____
_____

Today _____ helped me realize/learn/remember that _____
_____

Today I am very proud of myself for _____
_____
_____

I am going to bed grateful for today's day and:

1. _____
2. _____
3. _____
4. _____
5. _____

Good night _____, I love you.

Date _____

I woke up today feeling grateful for:

1._____

2._____

3._____

My wish for today is _____

_____ and I will let universe do its thing.

Affirmations:

I am _____

_____

_____

Today _____ helped me realize/learn/remember that _____
_____

Today I am very proud of myself for _____
_____
_____

I am going to bed grateful for today's day and:

1. _____
2. _____
3. _____
4. _____
5. _____

Good night _____, I love you.

Date _____

I woke up today feeling grateful for:

1. _____
2. _____
3. _____

My wish for today is _____
_____ and I will let universe do its thing.

Affirmations:

I am _____
_____
_____

Today _____ helped me realize/learn/remember that _____
_____

Today I am very proud of myself for _____
_____
_____

I am going to bed grateful for today's day and:

1. _____
2. _____
3. _____
4. _____
5. _____

Good night _____, I love you.

Date _____

I woke up today feeling grateful for:

1. _____
2. _____
3. _____

My wish for today is _____

_____ and I will let universe do its thing.

Affirmations:

I am _____

_____

_____

Today _____ helped me realize/learn/remember that _____
_____

Today I am very proud of myself for _____
_____
_____

I am going to bed grateful for today's day and:

1._____
2._____
3._____
4._____
5._____

Good night _____, I love you.

Date _____

I woke up today feeling grateful for:

1. _____
2. _____
3. _____

My wish for today is _____

_____ and I will let universe do its thing.

Affirmations:

I am _____

_____

_____

Today _____ helped me realize/learn/remember that _____
_____

Today I am very proud of myself for _____
_____
_____

I am going to bed grateful for today's day and:

1. _____

2. _____

3. _____

4. _____

5. _____

Good night _____, I love you.

Date _____

I woke up today feeling grateful for:

1. _____
2. _____
3. _____

My wish for today is _____

_____ and I will let universe do its thing.

Affirmations:

I am _____

_____

_____

Today _____ helped me realize/learn/remember

that _____

_____

Today I am very proud of myself for _____

_____

_____

I am going to bed grateful for today's day and:

1._____

2._____

3._____

4._____

5._____

Good night _____, I love you.

Date _____

I woke up today feeling grateful for:

1. _____
2. _____
3. _____

My wish for today is _____

_____ and I will let universe do its thing.

Affirmations:

I am _____

_____

_____

Today _____ helped me realize/learn/remember that _____
_____

Today I am very proud of myself for _____
_____
_____

I am going to bed grateful for today's day and:

1. _____

2. _____

3. _____

4. _____

5. _____

Good night _____, I love you.

Date _____

I woke up today feeling grateful for:

1. _____
2. _____
3. _____

My wish for today is _____

_____ and I will let universe do its thing.

Affirmations:

I am _____

_____

_____

Today _____ helped me realize/learn/remember that _____
_____

Today I am very proud of myself for _____
_____
_____

I am going to bed grateful for today's day and:

1._____
2._____
3._____
4._____
5._____

Good night _____, I love you.

Date _____

I woke up today feeling grateful for:

1. _____
2. _____
3. _____

My wish for today is _____

_____ and I will let universe do its thing.

Affirmations:

I am _____

_____

_____

Today _____ helped me realize/learn/remember that _____
_____

Today I am very proud of myself for _____

_____

_____

I am going to bed grateful for today's day and:

1._____

2._____

3._____

4._____

5._____

Good night _____, I love you.

Date _____

I woke up today feeling grateful for:

1. _____
2. _____
3. _____

My wish for today is _____
_____ and I will let universe do its thing.

Affirmations:

I am _____
_____
_____

Today _____ helped me realize/learn/remember that _____
_____

Today I am very proud of myself for _____
_____
_____

I am going to bed grateful for today's day and:

1. _____
2. _____
3. _____
4. _____
5. _____

Good night _____, I love you.

Date _____

I woke up today feeling grateful for:

1. _____

2. _____

3. _____

My wish for today is _____

_____ and I will let universe do its thing.

Affirmations:

I am _____

_____

_____

Today _____ helped me realize/learn/remember that _____
_____

Today I am very proud of myself for _____
_____
_____

I am going to bed grateful for today's day and:

1. _____
2. _____
3. _____
4. _____
5. _____

Good night _____, I love you.

Date _____

☼

I woke up today feeling grateful for:

1. _____

2. _____

3. _____

My wish for today is _____

_____ and I will let universe do its thing.

Affirmations:

I am _____

_____

_____

Today _____ helped me realize/learn/remember that _____
_____

Today I am very proud of myself for _____
_____
_____

I am going to bed grateful for today's day and:

1. _____
2. _____
3. _____
4. _____
5. _____

Good night _____, I love you.

Date _____

I woke up today feeling grateful for:

1. _____
2. _____
3. _____

My wish for today is _____
_____ and I will let universe do its thing.

Affirmations:

I am _____
_____
_____

Today _____ helped me realize/learn/remember that _____
_____

Today I am very proud of myself for _____
_____
_____

I am going to bed grateful for today's day and:

1. _____
2. _____
3. _____
4. _____
5. _____

Good night _____, I love you.

Date _____

☀

I woke up today feeling grateful for:

1. _____
2. _____
3. _____

My wish for today is _____
_____ and I will let universe do its thing.

Affirmations:

I am _____
_____
_____

Today _____ helped me realize/learn/remember that _____
_____

Today I am very proud of myself for _____
_____
_____

I am going to bed grateful for today's day and:

1. _____
2. _____
3. _____
4. _____
5. _____

Good night _____, I love you.

Date _____

I woke up today feeling grateful for:

1. _____
2. _____
3. _____

My wish for today is _____
_____ and I will let universe do its thing.

Affirmations:

I am _____
_____
_____

Today _____ helped me realize/learn/remember
that _____
_____

Today I am very proud of myself for _____
_____
_____

I am going to bed grateful for today's day and:

1. _____
2. _____
3. _____
4. _____
5. _____

Good night _____, I love you.

Date _____

I woke up today feeling grateful for:

1. _____
2. _____
3. _____

My wish for today is _____

_____ and I will let universe do its thing.

Affirmations:

I am _____

_____

_____

Today _____ helped me realize/learn/remember

that _____

_____

Today I am very proud of myself for _____

_____

_____

I am going to bed grateful for today's day and:

1. _____

2. _____

3. _____

4. _____

5. _____

Good night _____, I love you.

Date _____

I woke up today feeling grateful for:

1. _____
2. _____
3. _____

My wish for today is _____
_____ and I will let universe do its thing.

Affirmations:

I am _____
_____
_____

Today _____ helped me realize/learn/remember that _____
_____

Today I am very proud of myself for _____
_____
_____

I am going to bed grateful for today's day and:

1. _____
2. _____
3. _____
4. _____
5. _____

Good night _____, I love you.

Date _____

I woke up today feeling grateful for:

1._____
2._____
3._____

My wish for today is _____
_____ and I will let universe do its thing.

Affirmations:

I am _____
_____
_____

Today _____ helped me realize/learn/remember that _____
_____

Today I am very proud of myself for _____
_____
_____

I am going to bed grateful for today's day and:

1. _____
2. _____
3. _____
4. _____
5. _____

Good night _____, I love you.

Date _____

I woke up today feeling grateful for:

1. _____
2. _____
3. _____

My wish for today is _____

_____ and I will let universe do its thing.

Affirmations:

I am _____

_____

_____

Today _____ helped me realize/learn/remember that _____
_____

Today I am very proud of myself for _____
_____
_____

I am going to bed grateful for today's day and:

1. _____
2. _____
3. _____
4. _____
5. _____

Good night _____, I love you.

Date _____

I woke up today feeling grateful for:

1. _____
2. _____
3. _____

My wish for today is _____

_____ and I will let universe do its thing.

Affirmations:

I am _____

_____

_____

Today _____ helped me realize/learn/remember that _____
_____

Today I am very proud of myself for _____
_____
_____

I am going to bed grateful for today's day and:

1. _____
2. _____
3. _____
4. _____
5. _____

Good night _____, I love you.

Date _____

I woke up today feeling grateful for:

1. _____
2. _____
3. _____

My wish for today is _____

_____ and I will let universe do its thing.

Affirmations:

I am _____

_____

_____

Today _____ helped me realize/learn/remember that _____
_____

Today I am very proud of myself for _____

_____

_____

I am going to bed grateful for today's day and:

1._____

2._____

3._____

4._____

5._____

Good night _____, I love you.

Date _____

I woke up today feeling grateful for:

1. _____
2. _____
3. _____

My wish for today is _____

_____ and I will let universe do its thing.

Affirmations:

I am _____

_____

_____

Today _____ helped me realize/learn/remember that _____
_____

Today I am very proud of myself for _____
_____
_____

I am going to bed grateful for today's day and:

1. _____

2. _____

3. _____

4. _____

5. _____

Good night _____, I love you.

Date _____

I woke up today feeling grateful for:

1._____
2._____
3._____

My wish for today is _____

_____ and I will let universe do its thing.

Affirmations:

I am _____

_____

_____

Today _____ helped me realize/learn/remember that _____
_____

Today I am very proud of myself for _____
_____
_____

I am going to bed grateful for today's day and:

1._____

2._____

3._____

4._____

5._____

Good night _____, I love you.

Date _____

I woke up today feeling grateful for:

1. _____
2. _____
3. _____

My wish for today is _____

_____ and I will let universe do its thing.

Affirmations:

I am _____

_____

_____

Today _____ helped me realize/learn/remember that _____
_____

Today I am very proud of myself for _____
_____
_____

I am going to bed grateful for today's day and:

1. _____
2. _____
3. _____
4. _____
5. _____

Good night _____, I love you.

Date _____

I woke up today feeling grateful for:

1. _____
2. _____
3. _____

My wish for today is _____

_____ and I will let universe do its thing.

Affirmations:

I am _____

_____

_____

Today _____ helped me realize/learn/remember

that _____

_____

Today I am very proud of myself for _____

_____

_____

I am going to bed grateful for today's day and:

1._____

2._____

3._____

4._____

5._____

Good night _____, I love you.

Date _____

I woke up today feeling grateful for:

1. _____

2. _____

3. _____

My wish for today is _____

_____ and I will let universe do its thing.

Affirmations:

I am _____

_____

_____

Today _____ helped me realize/learn/remember that _____
_____

Today I am very proud of myself for _____
_____
_____

I am going to bed grateful for today's day and:

1._____

2._____

3._____

4._____

5._____

Good night _____, I love you.

Date _____

I woke up today feeling grateful for:

1. _____
2. _____
3. _____

My wish for today is _____
_____ and I will let universe do its thing.

Affirmations:

I am _____
_____
_____

Today _____ helped me realize/learn/remember that _____
_____

Today I am very proud of myself for _____
_____
_____

I am going to bed grateful for today's day and:

1. _____
2. _____
3. _____
4. _____
5. _____

Good night _____, I love you.

Date _____

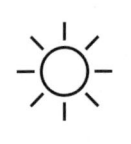

I woke up today feeling grateful for:

1._____

2._____

3._____

My wish for today is _____

_____ and I will let universe do its thing.

Affirmations:

I am _____

_____

_____

Today _____ helped me realize/learn/remember that _____
_____

Today I am very proud of myself for _____
_____
_____

I am going to bed grateful for today's day and:

1. _____
2. _____
3. _____
4. _____
5. _____

Good night _____, I love you.

Date _____

☀

I woke up today feeling grateful for:

1. _____
2. _____
3. _____

My wish for today is _____

_____ and I will let universe do its thing.

Affirmations:

I am _____

_____

_____

Today _____ helped me realize/learn/remember that _____
_____

Today I am very proud of myself for _____
_____
_____

I am going to bed grateful for today's day and:

1. _____
2. _____
3. _____
4. _____
5. _____

Good night _____, I love you.

Date _____

I woke up today feeling grateful for:

1. _____
2. _____
3. _____

My wish for today is _____

_____ and I will let universe do its thing.

Affirmations:

I am _____

_____

_____

Today _____ helped me realize/learn/remember

that _____

_____

Today I am very proud of myself for _____

_____

_____

I am going to bed grateful for today's day and:

1. _____

2. _____

3. _____

4. _____

5. _____

Good night _____, I love you.

Date _____

I woke up today feeling grateful for:

1. _____
2. _____
3. _____

My wish for today is _____

_____ and I will let universe do its thing.

Affirmations:

I am _____

_____

_____

Today _____ helped me realize/learn/remember that _____
_____

Today I am very proud of myself for _____
_____
_____

I am going to bed grateful for today's day and:

1._____
2._____
3._____
4._____
5._____

Good night _____, I love you.

Date _____

I woke up today feeling grateful for:

1. _____
2. _____
3. _____

My wish for today is _____

_____ and I will let universe do its thing.

Affirmations:

I am _____

_____

_____

Today _____ helped me realize/learn/remember that _____
_____

Today I am very proud of myself for _____
_____
_____

I am going to bed grateful for today's day and:

1._____
2._____
3._____
4._____
5._____

Good night _____, I love you.

Date _____

I woke up today feeling grateful for:

1. _____
2. _____
3. _____

My wish for today is _____

_____ and I will let universe do its thing.

Affirmations:

I am _____

_____

_____

Today _____ helped me realize/learn/remember that _____
_____

Today I am very proud of myself for _____
_____
_____

I am going to bed grateful for today's day and:

1. _____

2. _____

3. _____

4. _____

5. _____

Good night _____, I love you.

Date _____

I woke up today feeling grateful for:

1. _____
2. _____
3. _____

My wish for today is _____

_____ and I will let universe do its thing.

Affirmations:

I am _____

_____

_____

Today _____ helped me realize/learn/remember that _____
_____

Today I am very proud of myself for _____
_____
_____

I am going to bed grateful for today's day and:

1. _____
2. _____
3. _____
4. _____
5. _____

Good night _____, I love you.

Date _____

I woke up today feeling grateful for:

1._____
2._____
3._____

My wish for today is _____
_____ and I will let universe do its thing.

Affirmations:

I am _____
_____
_____

Today _____ helped me realize/learn/remember that _____
_____

Today I am very proud of myself for _____
_____
_____

I am going to bed grateful for today's day and:

1. _____
2. _____
3. _____
4. _____
5. _____

Good night _____, I love you.

Date _____

I woke up today feeling grateful for:

1. _____
2. _____
3. _____

My wish for today is _____
_____ and I will let universe do its thing.

Affirmations:

I am _____
_____
_____

Today _____ helped me realize/learn/remember that _____
_____

Today I am very proud of myself for _____
_____
_____

I am going to bed grateful for today's day and:

1. _____
2. _____
3. _____
4. _____
5. _____

Good night _____, I love you.

Date _____

I woke up today feeling grateful for:

1. _____

2. _____

3. _____

My wish for today is _____

_____ and I will let universe do its thing.

Affirmations:

I am _____

_____

_____

Today _____ helped me realize/learn/remember that _____
_____

Today I am very proud of myself for _____
_____
_____

I am going to bed grateful for today's day and:

1. _____
2. _____
3. _____
4. _____
5. _____

Good night _____, I love you.

Date _____

I woke up today feeling grateful for:

1. _____
2. _____
3. _____

My wish for today is _____
_____ and I will let universe do its thing.

Affirmations:

I am _____
_____
_____

Today _____ helped me realize/learn/remember that _____
_____

Today I am very proud of myself for _____
_____
_____

I am going to bed grateful for today's day and:

1. _____

2. _____

3. _____

4. _____

5. _____

Good night _____, I love you.

Date _____

I woke up today feeling grateful for:

1. _____
2. _____
3. _____

My wish for today is _____
_____ and I will let universe do its thing.

Affirmations:

I am _____
_____
_____

Today _____ helped me realize/learn/remember that _____
_____

Today I am very proud of myself for _____
_____
_____

I am going to bed grateful for today's day and:

1. _____
2. _____
3. _____
4. _____
5. _____

Good night _____, I love you.

Date _____

I woke up today feeling grateful for:

1. _____

2. _____

3. _____

My wish for today is _____

_____ and I will let universe do its thing.

Affirmations:

I am _____

_____

_____

Today _____ helped me realize/learn/remember that _____
_____

Today I am very proud of myself for _____
_____
_____

I am going to bed grateful for today's day and:

1. _____
2. _____
3. _____
4. _____
5. _____

Good night _____, I love you.

Date _____

☼

I woke up today feeling grateful for:

1. _____
2. _____
3. _____

My wish for today is _____

_____ and I will let universe do its thing.

Affirmations:

I am _____

_____

_____

Today _____ helped me realize/learn/remember that _____
_____

Today I am very proud of myself for _____
_____
_____

I am going to bed grateful for today's day and:

1. _____
2. _____
3. _____
4. _____
5. _____

Good night _____, I love you.

Date _____

I woke up today feeling grateful for:

1. _____

2. _____

3. _____

My wish for today is _____
_____ and I will let universe do its thing.

Affirmations:

I am _____
_____
_____

Today _____ helped me realize/learn/remember that _____
_____

Today I am very proud of myself for _____
_____
_____

I am going to bed grateful for today's day and:

1. _____
2. _____
3. _____
4. _____
5. _____

Good night _____, I love you.

Date _____

I woke up today feeling grateful for:

1. _____
2. _____
3. _____

My wish for today is _____

_____ and I will let universe do its thing.

Affirmations:

I am _____

_____

_____

Today _____ helped me realize/learn/remember that _____
_____

Today I am very proud of myself for _____
_____
_____

I am going to bed grateful for today's day and:

1. _____

2. _____

3. _____

4. _____

5. _____

Good night _____, I love you.

Date _____

I woke up today feeling grateful for:

1. _____
2. _____
3. _____

My wish for today is _____
_____ and I will let universe do its thing.

Affirmations:

I am _____
_____
_____

Today _____ helped me realize/learn/remember that _____
_____

Today I am very proud of myself for _____
_____
_____

I am going to bed grateful for today's day and:

1. _____
2. _____
3. _____
4. _____
5. _____

Good night _____, I love you.

Date _____

I woke up today feeling grateful for:

1. _____
2. _____
3. _____

My wish for today is _____

_____ and I will let universe do its thing.

Affirmations:

I am _____

_____

_____

Today _____ helped me realize/learn/remember that _____
_____

Today I am very proud of myself for _____
_____
_____

I am going to bed grateful for today's day and:

1. _____
2. _____
3. _____
4. _____
5. _____

Good night _____, I love you.

Date _____

I woke up today feeling grateful for:

1. _____
2. _____
3. _____

My wish for today is _____

_____ and I will let universe do its thing.

Affirmations:

I am _____

_____

_____

Today _____ helped me realize/learn/remember

that _____

_____

Today I am very proud of myself for _____

_____

_____

I am going to bed grateful for today's day and:

1._____

2._____

3._____

4._____

5._____

Good night _____, I love you.

Date _____

I woke up today feeling grateful for:

1. _____
2. _____
3. _____

My wish for today is _____

_____ and I will let universe do its thing.

Affirmations:

I am _____

_____

_____

Today _____ helped me realize/learn/remember that _____
_____

Today I am very proud of myself for _____
_____
_____

I am going to bed grateful for today's day and:

1. _____
2. _____
3. _____
4. _____
5. _____

Good night _____, I love you.

Date _____

I woke up today feeling grateful for:

1. _____
2. _____
3. _____

My wish for today is _____

_____ and I will let universe do its thing.

Affirmations:

I am _____

_____

_____

Today _____ helped me realize/learn/remember that _____
_____

Today I am very proud of myself for _____
_____
_____

I am going to bed grateful for today's day and:

1. _____
2. _____
3. _____
4. _____
5. _____

Good night _____, I love you.

Date _____

I woke up today feeling grateful for:

1. _____
2. _____
3. _____

My wish for today is _____

_____ and I will let universe do its thing.

Affirmations:

I am _____

_____

_____

Today _____ helped me realize/learn/remember that _____
_____

Today I am very proud of myself for _____
_____
_____

I am going to bed grateful for today's day and:

1. _____
2. _____
3. _____
4. _____
5. _____

Good night _____, I love you.

Date _____

I woke up today feeling grateful for:

1. _____
2. _____
3. _____

My wish for today is _____

_____ and I will let universe do its thing.

Affirmations:

I am _____

_____

_____

Today _____ helped me realize/learn/remember that _____
_____

Today I am very proud of myself for _____
_____
_____

I am going to bed grateful for today's day and:

1. _____
2. _____
3. _____
4. _____
5. _____

Good night _____, I love you.

Date _____

I woke up today feeling grateful for:

1. _____
2. _____
3. _____

My wish for today is _____

_____ and I will let universe do its thing.

Affirmations:

I am _____

_____

_____

Today _____ helped me realize/learn/remember that _____
_____

Today I am very proud of myself for _____
_____
_____

I am going to bed grateful for today's day and:

1. _____

2. _____

3. _____

4. _____

5. _____

Good night _____, I love you.

Date _____

I woke up today feeling grateful for:

1. _____
2. _____
3. _____

My wish for today is _____

_____ and I will let universe do its thing.

Affirmations:

I am _____

_____

_____

Today _____ helped me realize/learn/remember that _____
_____

Today I am very proud of myself for _____
_____
_____

I am going to bed grateful for today's day and:

1. _____
2. _____
3. _____
4. _____
5. _____

Good night _____, I love you.

Date _____

I woke up today feeling grateful for:

1. _____
2. _____
3. _____

My wish for today is _____
_____ and I will let universe do its thing.

Affirmations:

I am _____
_____
_____

Today _____ helped me realize/learn/remember

that _____

_____

Today I am very proud of myself for _____

_____

_____

I am going to bed grateful for today's day and:

1. _____

2. _____

3. _____

4. _____

5. _____

Good night _____, I love you.

Date _____

I woke up today feeling grateful for:

1. _____

2. _____

3. _____

My wish for today is _____

_____ and I will let universe do its thing.

Affirmations:

I am _____

_____

_____

Today _____ helped me realize/learn/remember that _____
_____

Today I am very proud of myself for _____
_____
_____

I am going to bed grateful for today's day and:

1._____

2._____

3._____

4._____

5._____

Good night _____, I love you.

Date _____

I woke up today feeling grateful for:

1. _____
2. _____
3. _____

My wish for today is _____
_____ and I will let universe do its thing.

Affirmations:

I am _____
_____
_____

Today _____ helped me realize/learn/remember that _____
_____

Today I am very proud of myself for _____
_____
_____

I am going to bed grateful for today's day and:

1. _____
2. _____
3. _____
4. _____
5. _____

Good night _____, I love you.

Date _____

I woke up today feeling grateful for:

1._____
2._____
3._____

My wish for today is _____

_____ and I will let universe do its thing.

Affirmations:

I am _____

_____

_____

Today _____ helped me realize/learn/remember that _____
_____

Today I am very proud of myself for _____

_____

_____

I am going to bed grateful for today's day and:

1._____
2._____
3._____
4._____
5._____

Good night _____, I love you.

Date _____

I woke up today feeling grateful for:

1. _____
2. _____
3. _____

My wish for today is _____
_____ and I will let universe do its thing.

Affirmations:

I am _____
_____
_____

Today _____ helped me realize/learn/remember that _____
_____

Today I am very proud of myself for _____
_____
_____

I am going to bed grateful for today's day and:

1._____
2._____
3._____
4._____
5._____

Good night _____, I love you.

Date _____

I woke up today feeling grateful for:

1. _____
2. _____
3. _____

My wish for today is _____

_____ and I will let universe do its thing.

Affirmations:

I am _____

_____

_____

Today _____ helped me realize/learn/remember that _____

_____

Today I am very proud of myself for _____

_____

_____

I am going to bed grateful for today's day and:

1. _____
2. _____
3. _____
4. _____
5. _____

Good night _____, I love you.

Date _____

I woke up today feeling grateful for:

1. _____
2. _____
3. _____

My wish for today is _____

_____ and I will let universe do its thing.

Affirmations:

I am _____

_____

_____

Today _____ helped me realize/learn/remember

that _____

_____

Today I am very proud of myself for _____

_____

_____

I am going to bed grateful for today's day and:

1. _____

2. _____

3. _____

4. _____

5. _____

Good night _____, I love you.

Date _____

I woke up today feeling grateful for:

1. _____
2. _____
3. _____

My wish for today is _____

_____ and I will let universe do its thing.

Affirmations:

I am _____

_____

_____

Today _____ helped me realize/learn/remember

that _____

_____

Today I am very proud of myself for _____

_____

_____

I am going to bed grateful for today's day and:

1._____

2._____

3._____

4._____

5._____

Good night _____, I love you.

Date _____

I woke up today feeling grateful for:

1. _____
2. _____
3. _____

My wish for today is _____

_____ and I will let universe do its thing.

Affirmations:

I am _____

_____

_____

Today _____ helped me realize/learn/remember

that _____

_____

Today I am very proud of myself for _____

_____

_____

I am going to bed grateful for today's day and:

1. _____

2. _____

3. _____

4. _____

5. _____

Good night _____, I love you.

Date _____

I woke up today feeling grateful for:

1. _____

2. _____

3. _____

My wish for today is _____

_____ and I will let universe do its thing.

Affirmations:

I am _____

_____

_____

Today _____ helped me realize/learn/remember that _____
_____

Today I am very proud of myself for _____
_____
_____

I am going to bed grateful for today's day and:

1. _____
2. _____
3. _____
4. _____
5. _____

Good night _____, I love you.

Date _____

I woke up today feeling grateful for:

1._____

2._____

3._____

My wish for today is _____

_____ and I will let universe do its thing.

Affirmations:

I am _____

_____

_____

Today _____ helped me realize/learn/remember

that _____

_____

Today I am very proud of myself for _____

_____

_____

I am going to bed grateful for today's day and:

1. _____

2. _____

3. _____

4. _____

5. _____

Good night _____, I love you.

Date _____

I woke up today feeling grateful for:

1._____

2._____

3._____

My wish for today is _____

_____ and I will let universe do its thing.

Affirmations:

I am _____

_____

_____

Today _____ helped me realize/learn/remember

that _____

_____

Today I am very proud of myself for _____

_____

_____

I am going to bed grateful for today's day and:

1._____

2._____

3._____

4._____

5._____

Good night _____, I love you.

Date _____

I woke up today feeling grateful for:

1. _____
2. _____
3. _____

My wish for today is _____

_____ and I will let universe do its thing.

Affirmations:

I am _____

_____

_____

Today _____ helped me realize/learn/remember

that _____

_____

Today I am very proud of myself for _____

_____

_____

I am going to bed grateful for today's day and:

1. _____

2. _____

3. _____

4. _____

5. _____

Good night _____, I love you.

Date _____

I woke up today feeling grateful for:

1. _____
2. _____
3. _____

My wish for today is _____

_____ and I will let universe do its thing.

Affirmations:

I am _____

_____

_____

Today _____ helped me realize/learn/remember

that _____

_____

Today I am very proud of myself for _____

_____

_____

I am going to bed grateful for today's day and:

1._____

2._____

3._____

4._____

5._____

Good night _____, I love you.

Date _____

I woke up today feeling grateful for:

1._____
2._____
3._____

My wish for today is _____

_____ and I will let universe do its thing.

Affirmations:

I am _____

_____

_____

Today _____ helped me realize/learn/remember

that _____

_____

Today I am very proud of myself for _____

_____

_____

I am going to bed grateful for today's day and:

1._____

2._____

3._____

4._____

5._____

Good night _____, I love you.

Date _____

I woke up today feeling grateful for:

1. _____

2. _____

3. _____

My wish for today is _____

_____ and I will let universe do its thing.

Affirmations:

I am _____

_____

_____

Today _____ helped me realize/learn/remember that _____
_____

Today I am very proud of myself for _____
_____
_____

I am going to bed grateful for today's day and:

1._____
2._____
3._____
4._____
5._____

Good night _____, I love you.

Date _____

I woke up today feeling grateful for:

1. _____
2. _____
3. _____

My wish for today is _____
_____ and I will let universe do its thing.

Affirmations:

I am _____
_____
_____

Today _____ helped me realize/learn/remember

that _____

_____

Today I am very proud of myself for _____

_____

_____

I am going to bed grateful for today's day and:

1. _____

2. _____

3. _____

4. _____

5. _____

Good night _____, I love you.

Date _____

I woke up today feeling grateful for:

1._____

2._____

3._____

My wish for today is _____
_____ and I will let universe do its thing.

Affirmations:

I am _____
_____
_____

Today _____ helped me realize/learn/remember
that _____
_____

Today I am very proud of myself for _____
_____
_____

I am going to bed grateful for today's day and:

1. _____

2. _____

3. _____

4. _____

5. _____

Good night _____, I love you.

Date _____

I woke up today feeling grateful for:

1._____
2._____
3._____

My wish for today is _____

_____ and I will let universe do its thing.

Affirmations:

I am _____

_____

_____

Today _____ helped me realize/learn/remember that _____
_____

Today I am very proud of myself for _____
_____
_____

I am going to bed grateful for today's day and:

1. _____
2. _____
3. _____
4. _____
5. _____

Good night _____, I love you.

Date _____

I woke up today feeling grateful for:

1. _____
2. _____
3. _____

My wish for today is _____

_____ and I will let universe do its thing.

Affirmations:

I am _____

_____

_____

Today _____ helped me realize/learn/remember

that _____

_____

Today I am very proud of myself for _____

_____

_____

I am going to bed grateful for today's day and:

1. _____
2. _____
3. _____
4. _____
5. _____

Good night _____, I love you.

Date _____

I woke up today feeling grateful for:

1. _____
2. _____
3. _____

My wish for today is _____

_____ and I will let universe do its thing.

Affirmations:

I am _____

_____

_____

Today _____ helped me realize/learn/remember

that _____

_____

Today I am very proud of myself for _____

_____

_____

I am going to bed grateful for today's day and:

1._____

2._____

3._____

4._____

5._____

Good night _____, I love you.

Date _____

I woke up today feeling grateful for:

1. _____

2. _____

3. _____

My wish for today is _____

_____ and I will let universe do its thing.

Affirmations:

I am _____

_____

_____

Today _____ helped me realize/learn/remember that _____
_____

Today I am very proud of myself for _____

_____

_____

I am going to bed grateful for today's day and:

1. _____
2. _____
3. _____
4. _____
5. _____

Good night _____, I love you.

Date _____

I woke up today feeling grateful for:

1._____

2._____

3._____

My wish for today is _____

_____ and I will let universe do its thing.

Affirmations:

I am _____

_____

_____

Today _____ helped me realize/learn/remember that _____
_____

Today I am very proud of myself for _____
_____
_____

I am going to bed grateful for today's day and:

1. _____

2. _____

3. _____

4. _____

5. _____

Good night _____, I love you.

Date _____

I woke up today feeling grateful for:

1. _____
2. _____
3. _____

My wish for today is _____

_____ and I will let universe do its thing.

Affirmations:

I am _____

_____

_____

Today _____ helped me realize/learn/remember that _____
_____

Today I am very proud of myself for _____
_____
_____

I am going to bed grateful for today's day and:

1. _____
2. _____
3. _____
4. _____
5. _____

Good night _____, I love you.

Date _____

I woke up today feeling grateful for:

1. _____
2. _____
3. _____

My wish for today is _____

_____ and I will let universe do its thing.

Affirmations:

I am _____

_____

_____

Today _____ helped me realize/learn/remember that _____
_____

Today I am very proud of myself for _____
_____
_____

I am going to bed grateful for today's day and:

1. _____
2. _____
3. _____
4. _____
5. _____

Good night _____, I love you.

Date _____

I woke up today feeling grateful for:

1. _____
2. _____
3. _____

My wish for today is _____
_____ and I will let universe do its thing.

Affirmations:

I am _____
_____
_____

Today _____ helped me realize/learn/remember that _____
_____

Today I am very proud of myself for _____
_____
_____

I am going to bed grateful for today's day and:

1. _____
2. _____
3. _____
4. _____
5. _____

Good night _____, I love you.

Date _____

I woke up today feeling grateful for:

1. _____
2. _____
3. _____

My wish for today is _____

_____ and I will let universe do its thing.

Affirmations:

I am _____

_____

_____

Today _____ helped me realize/learn/remember

that _____

_____

Today I am very proud of myself for _____

_____

_____

I am going to bed grateful for today's day and:

1._____

2._____

3._____

4._____

5._____

Good night _____, I love you.

Date _____

I woke up today feeling grateful for:

1. _____
2. _____
3. _____

My wish for today is _____

_____ and I will let universe do its thing.

Affirmations:

I am _____

_____

_____

Today _____ helped me realize/learn/remember that _____
_____

Today I am very proud of myself for _____
_____
_____

I am going to bed grateful for today's day and:

1. _____
2. _____
3. _____
4. _____
5. _____

Good night _____, I love you.

Date _____

I woke up today feeling grateful for:

1. _____
2. _____
3. _____

My wish for today is _____
_____ and I will let universe do its thing.

Affirmations:

I am _____
_____
_____

Today _____ helped me realize/learn/remember that _____
_____

Today I am very proud of myself for _____
_____
_____

I am going to bed grateful for today's day and:

1. _____
2. _____
3. _____
4. _____
5. _____

Good night _____, I love you.

Date _____

I woke up today feeling grateful for:

1. _____
2. _____
3. _____

My wish for today is _____

_____ and I will let universe do its thing.

Affirmations:

I am _____

_____

_____

Today _____ helped me realize/learn/remember

that _____

_____

Today I am very proud of myself for _____

_____

_____

I am going to bed grateful for today's day and:

1. _____

2. _____

3. _____

4. _____

5. _____

Good night _____, I love you.

Date _____

I woke up today feeling grateful for:

1._____
2._____
3._____

My wish for today is _____
_____ and I will let universe do its thing.

Affirmations:

I am _____
_____
_____

Today _____ helped me realize/learn/remember that _____
_____

Today I am very proud of myself for _____
_____
_____

I am going to bed grateful for today's day and:

1. _____
2. _____
3. _____
4. _____
5. _____

Good night _____, I love you.

Date _____

I woke up today feeling grateful for:

1._____

2._____

3._____

My wish for today is _____

_____ and I will let universe do its thing.

Affirmations:

I am _____

_____

_____

Today _____ helped me realize/learn/remember

that _____

_____

Today I am very proud of myself for _____

_____

_____

I am going to bed grateful for today's day and:

1. _____

2. _____

3. _____

4. _____

5. _____

Good night _____, I love you.

Date _____

I woke up today feeling grateful for:

1. _____

2. _____

3. _____

My wish for today is _____

_____ and I will let universe do its thing.

Affirmations:

I am _____

_____

_____

Today _____ helped me realize/learn/remember that _____
_____

Today I am very proud of myself for _____
_____
_____

I am going to bed grateful for today's day and:

1. _____
2. _____
3. _____
4. _____
5. _____

Good night _____, I love you.

Date _____

I woke up today feeling grateful for:

1. _____
2. _____
3. _____

My wish for today is _____

_____ and I will let universe do its thing.

Affirmations:

I am _____

_____

_____

Today _____ helped me realize/learn/remember that _____
_____

Today I am very proud of myself for _____
_____
_____

I am going to bed grateful for today's day and:

1._____

2._____

3._____

4._____

5._____

Good night _____, I love you.

Date _____

I woke up today feeling grateful for:

1. _____
2. _____
3. _____

My wish for today is _____

_____ and I will let universe do its thing.

Affirmations:

I am _____

_____

_____

Today _____ helped me realize/learn/remember that _____
_____

Today I am very proud of myself for _____
_____
_____

I am going to bed grateful for today's day and:

1._____

2._____

3._____

4._____

5._____

Good night _____, I love you.

Date _____

I woke up today feeling grateful for:

1. _____
2. _____
3. _____

My wish for today is _____

_____ and I will let universe do its thing.

Affirmations:

I am _____

_____

_____

Today _____ helped me realize/learn/remember that _____
_____

Today I am very proud of myself for _____
_____
_____

I am going to bed grateful for today's day and:

1._____

2._____

3._____

4._____

5._____

Good night _____, I love you.

Date _____

I woke up today feeling grateful for:

1. _____
2. _____
3. _____

My wish for today is _____

_____ and I will let universe do its thing.

Affirmations:

I am _____

_____

_____

Today _____ helped me realize/learn/remember that _____
_____

Today I am very proud of myself for _____
_____
_____

I am going to bed grateful for today's day and:

1. _____

2. _____

3. _____

4. _____

5. _____

Good night _____, I love you.

Date _____

I woke up today feeling grateful for:

1. _____
2. _____
3. _____

My wish for today is _____

_____ and I will let universe do its thing.

Affirmations:

I am _____

_____

_____

Today _____ helped me realize/learn/remember that _____
_____

Today I am very proud of myself for _____
_____
_____

I am going to bed grateful for today's day and:

1. _____
2. _____
3. _____
4. _____
5. _____

Good night _____, I love you.

Date _____

I woke up today feeling grateful for:

1. _____
2. _____
3. _____

My wish for today is _____

_____ and I will let universe do its thing.

Affirmations:

I am _____

_____

_____

Today _____ helped me realize/learn/remember

that _____

_____

Today I am very proud of myself for _____

_____

_____

I am going to bed grateful for today's day and:

1._____

2._____

3._____

4._____

5._____

Good night _____, I love you.

Date _____

I woke up today feeling grateful for:

1. _____
2. _____
3. _____

My wish for today is _____

_____ and I will let universe do its thing.

Affirmations:

I am _____

_____

_____

Today _____ helped me realize/learn/remember that _____
_____

Today I am very proud of myself for _____
_____
_____

I am going to bed grateful for today's day and:

1. _____
2. _____
3. _____
4. _____
5. _____

Good night _____, I love you.

Date _____

I woke up today feeling grateful for:

1._____
2._____
3._____

My wish for today is _____
_____ and I will let universe do its thing.

Affirmations:

I am _____
_____
_____

Today _____ helped me realize/learn/remember

that _____

_____

Today I am very proud of myself for _____

_____

_____

I am going to bed grateful for today's day and:

1. _____

2. _____

3. _____

4. _____

5. _____

Good night _____, I love you.

Date _____

I woke up today feeling grateful for:

1._____
2._____
3._____

My wish for today is _____
_____ and I will let universe do its thing.

Affirmations:

I am _____
_____
_____

Today _____ helped me realize/learn/remember that _____
_____

Today I am very proud of myself for _____
_____
_____

I am going to bed grateful for today's day and:

1._____
2._____
3._____
4._____
5._____

Good night _____, I love you.

Date _____

I woke up today feeling grateful for:

1. _____
2. _____
3. _____

My wish for today is _____

_____ and I will let universe do its thing.

Affirmations:

I am _____

_____

_____

Today _____ helped me realize/learn/remember that _____
_____

Today I am very proud of myself for _____
_____
_____

I am going to bed grateful for today's day and:

1. _____

2. _____

3. _____

4. _____

5. _____

Good night _____, I love you.

Date _____

I woke up today feeling grateful for:

1. _____
2. _____
3. _____

My wish for today is _____

_____ and I will let universe do its thing.

Affirmations:

I am _____

_____

_____

Today _____ helped me realize/learn/remember that _____
_____

Today I am very proud of myself for _____
_____
_____

I am going to bed grateful for today's day and:

1. _____
2. _____
3. _____
4. _____
5. _____

Good night _____, I love you.

Date _____

I woke up today feeling grateful for:

1. _____

2. _____

3. _____

My wish for today is _____

_____ and I will let universe do its thing.

Affirmations:

I am _____

_____

_____

Today _____ helped me realize/learn/remember

that _____

_____

Today I am very proud of myself for _____

_____

_____

I am going to bed grateful for today's day and:

1. _____

2. _____

3. _____

4. _____

5. _____

Good night _____, I love you.

Beliefs that don't serve me anymore:

New beliefs that are serving me NOW:

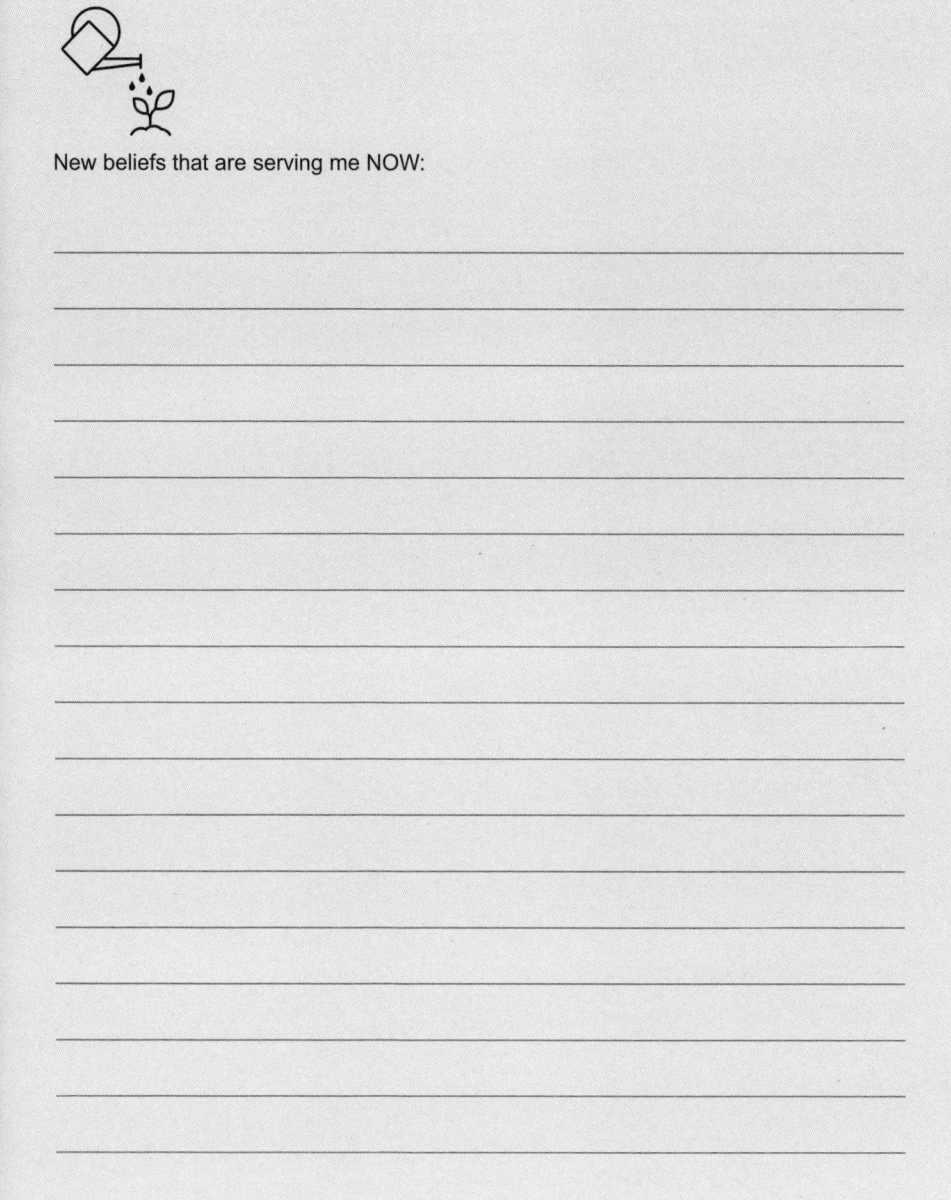

Beliefs that don't serve me anymore:

_____
_____
_____
_____
_____
_____
_____
_____
_____
_____
_____
_____
_____
_____
_____
_____
_____
_____

New beliefs that are serving me NOW:

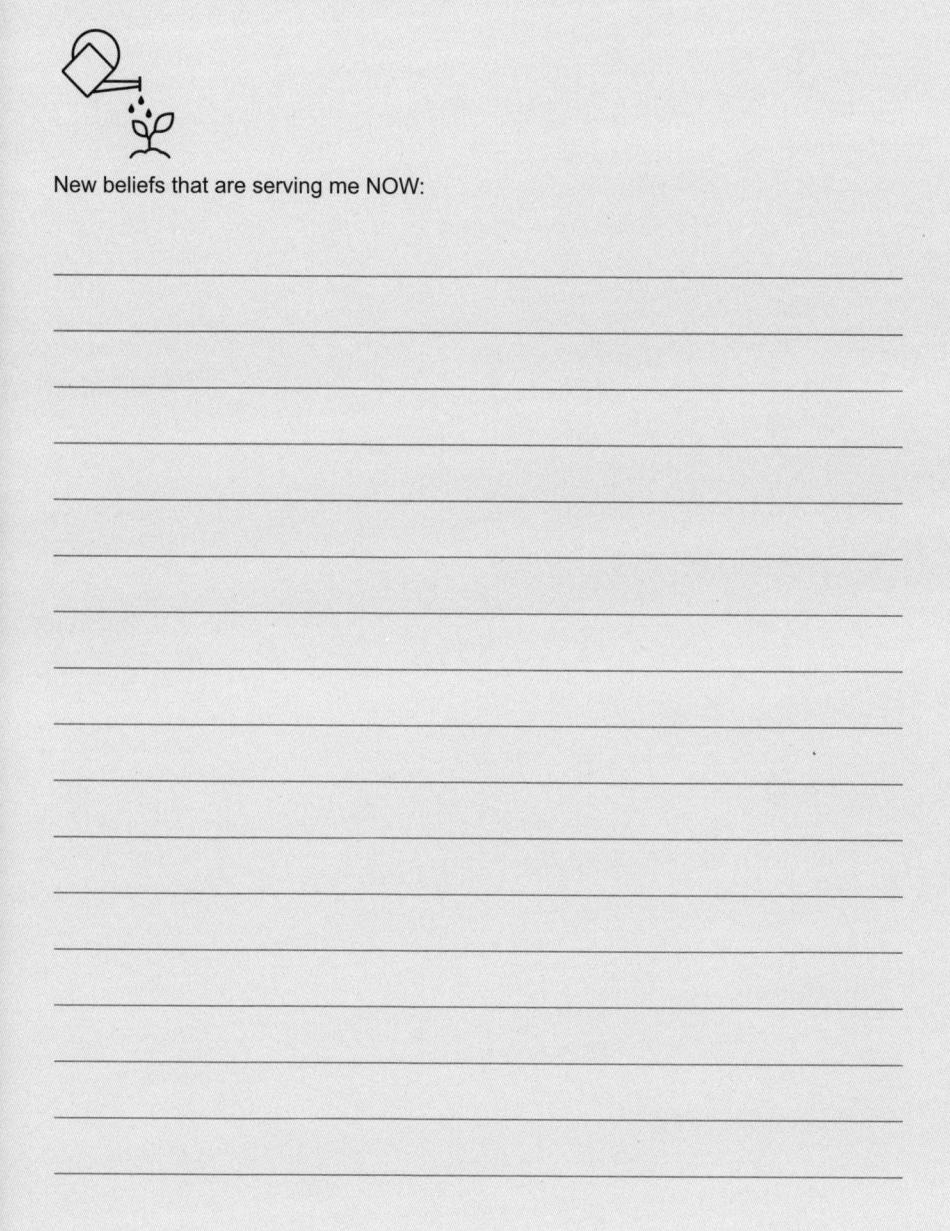

Beliefs that don't serve me anymore:

_____
_____
_____
_____
_____
_____
_____
_____
_____
_____
_____
_____
_____
_____
_____
_____
_____

New beliefs that are serving me NOW:

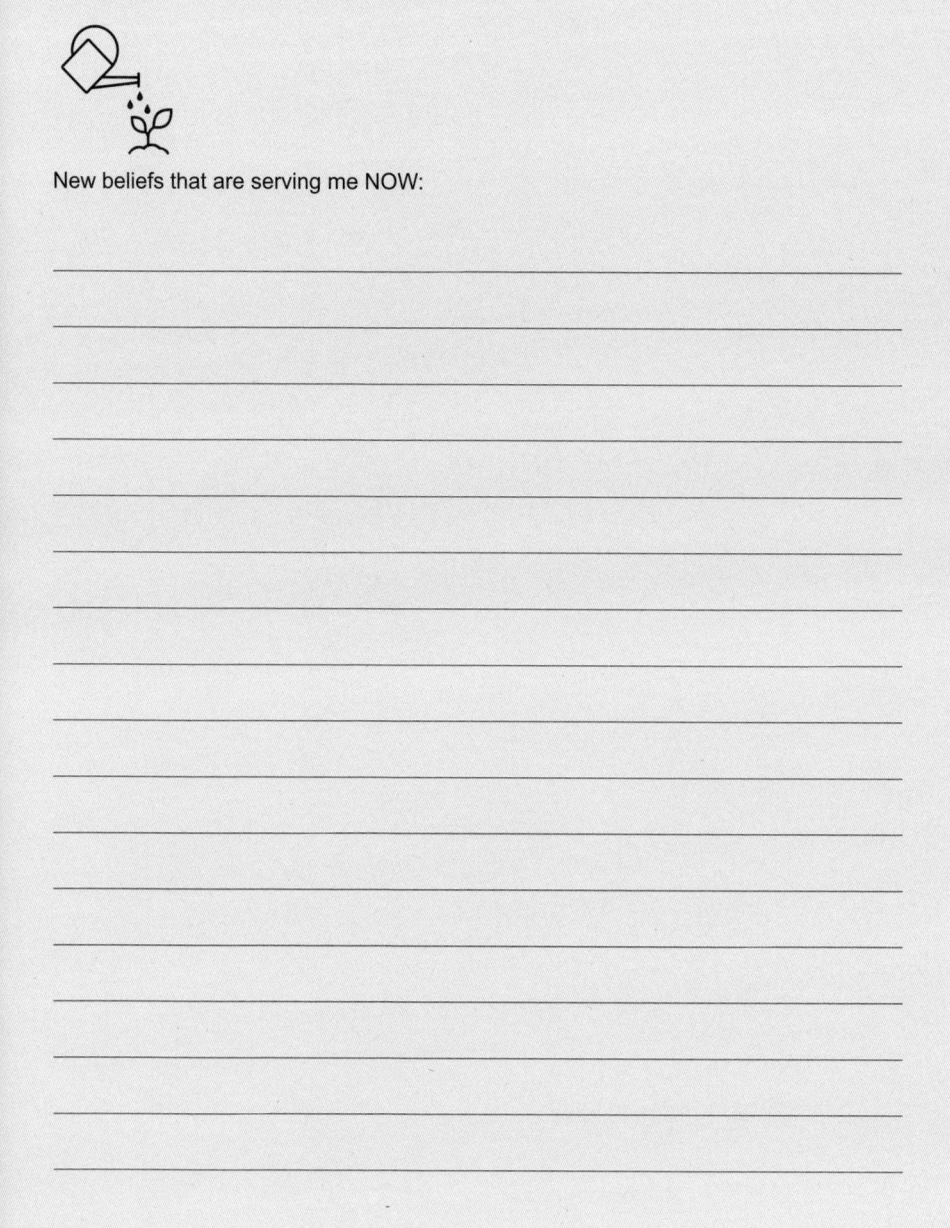

Beliefs that don't serve me anymore:

New beliefs that are serving me NOW:

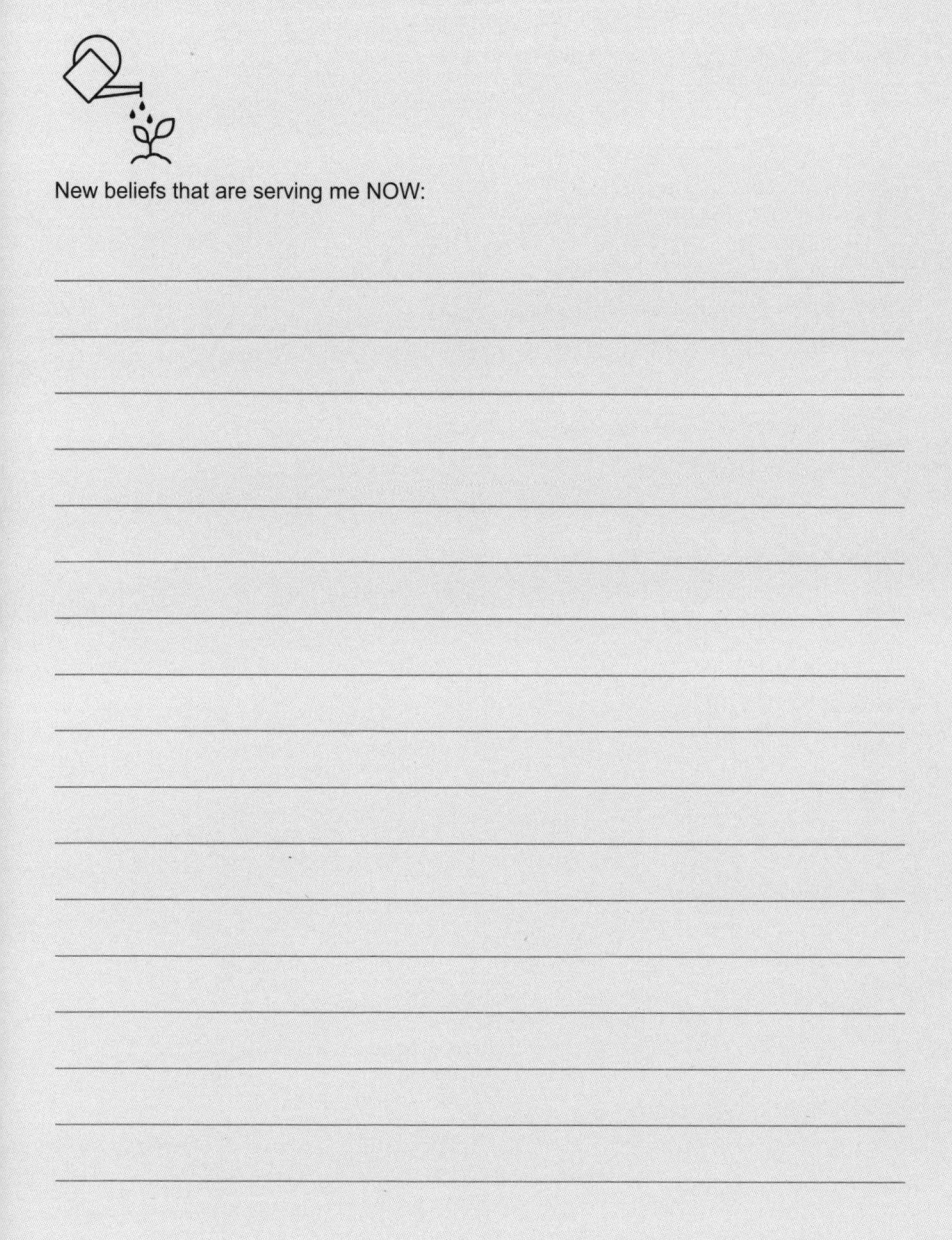

Beliefs that don't serve me anymore:

New beliefs that are serving me NOW:

Beliefs that don't serve me anymore:

New beliefs that are serving me NOW:

Beliefs that don't serve me anymore:

_____

_____

_____

_____

_____

_____

_____

_____

_____

_____

_____

_____

_____

_____

_____

_____

_____

New beliefs that are serving me NOW:

Beliefs that don't serve me anymore:

New beliefs that are serving me NOW:

Beliefs that don't serve me anymore:

_____
_____
_____
_____
_____
_____
_____
_____
_____
_____
_____
_____
_____
_____
_____
_____

New beliefs that are serving me NOW:

Beliefs that don't serve me anymore:

_____
_____
_____
_____
_____
_____
_____
_____
_____
_____
_____
_____
_____
_____
_____

New beliefs that are serving me NOW:

Beliefs that don't serve me anymore:

New beliefs that are serving me NOW:

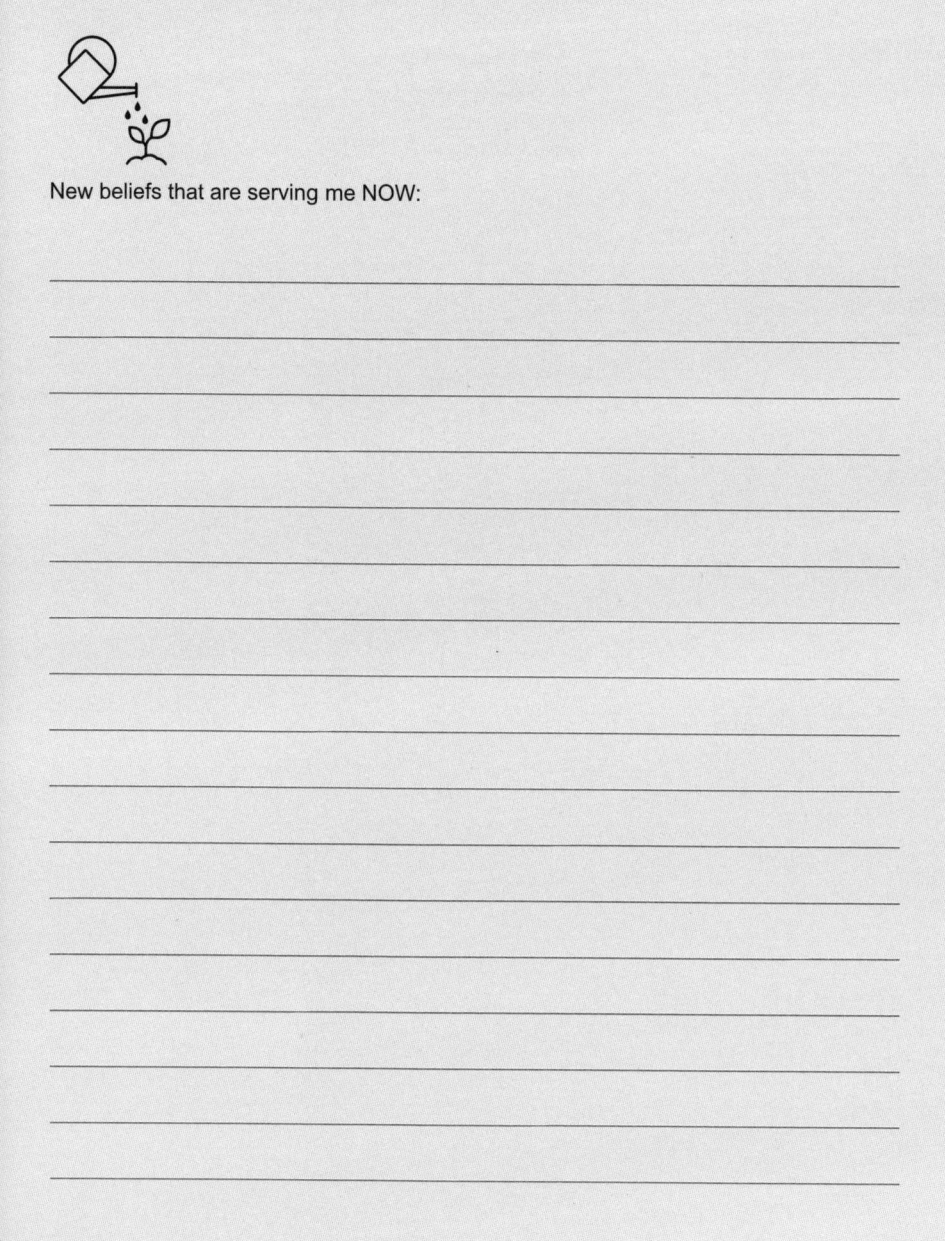

Page of positive aspects

Page of positive aspects

Page of positive aspects

Page of positive aspects

Page of positive aspects

Page of positive aspects

Page of positive aspects

Page of positive aspects

Page of positive aspects

Page of positive aspects

Page of positive aspects

Page of positive aspects

It's happening

It's happening

It's happening

It's happening

It's happening

It's happening

It's happening

It's happening

It's happening

It's happening

It's happening

It's happening

It's happening

It's happening

It's happening

It's happening

It's happening

It's happening

It's happening

It's happening

It's happening

It's happening

What do I want?
Why do I want it?

What do I want?
Why do I want it?

What do I want?
Why do I want it?

What do I want?
Why do I want it?

What do I want?
Why do I want it?

What do I want?
Why do I want it?

What do I want?
Why do I want it?

What do I want?
Why do I want it?

What do I want?
Why do I want it?

What do I want?
Why do I want it?

What do I want?
Why do I want it?

What do I want?
Why do I want it?

What do I want?
Why do I want it?

What do I want?
Why do I want it?

Letter to: _____

Letter to: _____

Letter to: _____

Letter to: _____

Letter to: _____

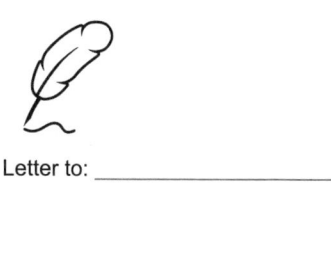

Letter to: _____

Letter to: _____

Letter to: _____

Letter to: _____

Letter to: _____

Letter to: _____

Letter to: _____

Letter to: _____

Letter to: _____

I forgive you …

I forgive you …

I forgive you …

I forgive you …

I forgive you …

I forgive you …

I forgive you …

I forgive you …

I forgive you …

I forgive you …

I forgive you …

I forgive you …

I forgive you …

I forgive you …